RICHARD HAL

VIKING AGE ARCHAEOLOGY
IN BRITAIN AND IRELAND

SHIRE ARCHAEOLOGY

2

Cover photograph
Ninth-century boat grave at Westness, Rousay, Orkney: a man buried with
weapons including sword, spear, axe, arrows and shield, and an adze, honestone,
strike-a-light and flints. The boat is 4.5 metres (14 feet 9 inches) long.
(Photograph: Sigrid Kaland.)

British Library Cataloguing in Publication Data:
Hall, Richard, *1949-*
Viking age archaeology in Britain and Ireland.
— (Shire archaeology; V.60).
1. Great Britain. Viking antiquities. Excavation of remains.
2. Ireland. Viking antiquities. Excavation of remains.
I. Title
941.01
ISBN 0-7478-0063-4

Published in 1995 by
SHIRE PUBLICATIONS LTD
Cromwell House, Church Street, Princes Risborough,
Buckinghamshire HP27 9AA, UK.

Series Editor: James Dyer

ISBN 0 7478 0063 4.

First published 1990; reprinted with amendments 1995.

Printed in Great Britain by
CIT Printing Services, Press Buildings,
Merlins Bridge, Haverfordwest, Dyfed SA61 1XF.

Contents

List of illustrations

Acknowledgements

I am grateful to the following for their help in obtaining illustrations: Paul Bennett, Martin Biddle, Glenys Boyles, Debbie Caulfield, Rosemary Cramp, Simon Hill, Sheena Howarth, Ross Trench-Jellicoe, Sigrid Kaland, Jim Lang, Chris Morris, Alison Sheridan, Pat Wallace, the late Dudley Waterman, Leslie Webster and York Archaeological Trust.

1
Introduction

The Vikings were sea-rovers and plunderers from Scandinavia who launched attacks all along the coastline of the British Isles and into a great many parts of its interior. These attacks, and the subsequent immigration and settlement, were part of a wider movement which took Scandinavians along the European coast and into the Mediterranean, westwards across the Atlantic, and eastwards from the Baltic into Russia. The first Viking raids in the British Isles to be recorded by their horrified victims took place just before AD 800. They were hit-and-run affairs, directed against potentially lucrative but weakly defended coastal or island sites, principally monasteries. When the opposition had been sized up, a second wave of attacks led to permanent settlement in some parts of the British Isles, although the speed with which raiding turned to immigration varied from area to area. Only Wales seems to have deterred permanent occupation on any significant scale. Subsequently, although there was important settlement in Scotland and the Isle of Man, the best known political events took place in the wealthier England and Ireland, where two rather different types of Viking occupation and settlement had taken place; these areas continued to be contested between native and newcomer, sometimes with fresh injections of direct Scandinavian interest, until the eleventh century.

The Viking age is normally thought of as ending in the mid eleventh century. In England the death of the last great Viking age leader, Harald Hardraada, and the subsequent victory by William the Conqueror, the descendant of a Viking settler in Normandy, conveniently signal the end of the era. There were, however, later manifestations of Scandinavian interest in the British Isles. Although under close Irish supervision, Dublin remained a Norse port until its capture by the invading Normans in 1170; the Western Isles of Scotland and the Isle of Man remained under Scandinavian authority until 1266, and Orkney and Shetland belonged to the King of Norway as late as 1469.

This book attempts to introduce the archaeology of the Viking raiders and Scandinavian immigrants throughout the British Isles (figure 1). It concentrates on those elements of their archaeological remains which are distinctively Scandinavian and largely bypasses the elements which they adopted or adapted from the indigenous inhabitants. Thus, although a variety of crafts and

1. Principal sites referred to in this book. The dotted line marks the southern limit of the English Danelaw. (Drawn by G. Boyles.)

industries flourished in the urban settlements which they developed, particularly in England, many of these, such as pottery making or the manufacture of iron tools, which do not show specifically Scandinavian influences or characteristics, are ignored.

The archaeological remains of these Norse newcomers are very varied, consisting principally of rural settlements, stone-carving, graves, silver hoards and town sites. These differing forms of evidence help to throw light on a variety of aspects of the Viking and Scandinavian impact, but they are not evenly spread across the chronological and geographical range of Norse activities. Some have been discovered very recently, and both they and the earlier finds are the subject of continuing research, analysis and re-evaluation. Viking age archaeology is a healthy and growing subject, and some aspects, such as the archaeology of the effect of the Vikings on their unwilling hosts, have had to be omitted, as has any attempt at a continuous historical narrative.

2
Early studies of the Vikings

British scholars from the sixteenth century onwards have been in no doubt of the Viking or Scandinavian impact on the country-side. Daniel Defoe, for example, could write:

'......... with easy search you may discern
Your Roman, Saxon, Danish, Norman, English ...'

In England the flowering of Anglo-Saxon studies *c.*1660-1730 reawakened appreciation of contemporary texts like the Anglo-Saxon Chronicle which took the Viking invasions as a main theme, and in the countryside many features were identified as being of Viking origin. Among them were what are now known to be early prehistoric monuments such as Stonehenge and numerous other lesser stone circles. Many earthworks too were attributed to the Vikings, some of them because they were called Danes Camp or some such name. The Danes Camps can still be found on maps although none can be linked convincingly to a Viking origin; in fairness to the antiquarians, they were not to know that these names sometimes developed through a standard linguistic change to an original Old English component *dene*, meaning a valley.

Perhaps the first remains of Norse origin to be correctly identified in Britain were the coins they issued there. Some of these bore the names of the kings who controlled their minting, and sometimes they could be equated with kings mentioned in the annals of the Anglo-Saxon Chronicle; thus the date of the coins could be established. In turn they could be used to provide an indication of the date of any other items buried with them — usually intact or broken-up silver jewellery, the latter known as hacksilver. Such silver hoards, found during agricultural operations and road and canal building, naturally excited widespread comment, and there was some chance of recovering the objects before they were dispersed and melted down.

Another sort of discovery to excite antiquarian interest was any grave containing a skeleton accompanied by objects. Such finds can be of almost any period, and it was only in the nineteenth century, when Viking age objects from the Scandinavian homelands were becoming better known in Britain, that Viking burials could be correctly identified (figure 2).

It was, then, coins, associated silver jewellery and accompanied burials which were the focus of study for anti-

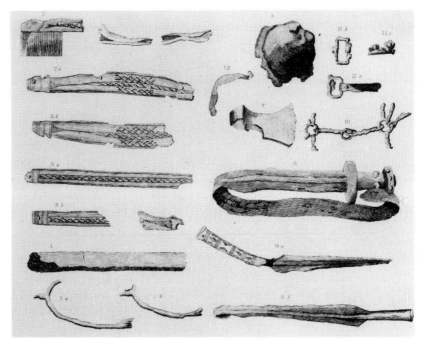

2. Hesket in the Forest, Cumbria: the original illustration from *Archaeologia Aeliana* II, 1832, of objects discovered in 1822 in a Viking grave: 1-3, antler comb fragments; 4, whetstone; 5, spurs; 6, shield boss; 7, axe; 8, sword; 9, spearheads; 10, bridle; 11, buckles; 12, iron fragment. (Photograph: K. Buck.)

quarians interested in the Viking age in Britain and Ireland. Increasingly, chance finds of objects of recognisably Scandinavian type or Viking age date, like those discovered in York in the later nineteenth and twentieth centuries, could also be attributed to Scandinavian intervention or settlement. Fieldwork and excavation at this time concentrated largely on the more obvious and identifiable Roman, prehistoric or later medieval remains, and apart from a handful of exceptions it is only since the 1950s that a few of the rural and urban settlements of the Norse in Britain have been discovered and excavated.

3
The first raids

The voyages to Britain and Ireland, which were to create such initial mayhem and ultimately to have such far reaching consequences, were possible because of the Scandinavians' mastery of shipbuilding, sailing and navigation. Crucial was the adoption of the sail, an event of the seventh and eighth centuries, which broadened the range of Scandinavian maritime endeavours and put Orkney and Shetland, some 350 km (220 miles) from the west coast of Norway, within a few days sailing on the spring easterly winds, with a return in the autumn facilitated by that season's westerlies.

No classic Viking shallow-draught longship or warship, which would have been used for raiding, has yet been found in Britain or Ireland. Nor has any merchantman or trading vessel, with a greater draught and capacity if less manoeuvrability, which would have been most suitable for transporting families and their possessions across the North Sea. The biggest vessels found in the British Isles, surviving only as soil-stains or concentrations of boat nails in elaborate burials in the Isle of Man and the Scottish isles, were about 11 metres (36 feet) long. They probably had four pairs of oars and may have been fishing smacks. They would have been capable of making the voyage from Scandinavia to Britain but are almost certainly not the vessels used by the early Viking raiders or Scandinavian immigrants.

In theory, at least, the first hit-and-run summer raids could have left archaeological remains in the form of destroyed buildings and hoards of valuables or coins buried for safety and not recovered; there might also be the graves of either Vikings or their victims. In each of these cases, however, there is an archaeological problem. In the first place it is difficult to date most surviving archaeological remains of this era with confidence to within, say, 25 years on either side; and secondly, even where greater precision is possible, normally because of the discovery of associated coins, it is usually speculative to link such remains positively to Viking action. In any case, perhaps the raids were not always so devastating as we allow ourselves to think — after all, the monks of Lindisfarne, Northumberland, who suffered a well reported raid in 793, were able to keep intact the famous coffin reliquary of St Cuthbert.

Although some of the places — mainly monasteries — that

were attacked in the first Viking raids are listed in contemporary historical sources, unequivocal traces of Viking destruction have not been identified archaeologically at any of them. It used to be thought that some of these sites ceased to function in later centuries because of the debilitating effects of Viking attack or Scandinavian settlement. Recent excavations cast doubt on this idea, however, for they have shown that some, like Hartlepool, Cleveland, apparently ceased to function before the Viking raids, while at others, such as Jarrow and Monkwearmouth, both Tyne and Wear, there obviously was some continuing ecclesiastical presence in the later Anglo-Saxon period. On the other hand, there is some historical evidence for the impact of the raids — for example, they did bring about the transfer of many monks from the Hebridean island of Iona to Kells, County Meath, in 807, and they also led to the abandonment of Lindisfarne by the Cuthbert community in 875.

The smash-and-grab tactics of these early raids did not often lead to battles, and no camp sites, burial grounds or individual graves can be firmly attributed to the Viking raids of the early ninth century. There are, however, many Viking graves in the British Isles which contain weapons of standard Viking age types, and, whatever their precise date, they serve to introduce the typical array of weapons used by Viking raiders.

Weapons

The most elaborate, costly and prestigious item was a double-edged iron sword, often carefully fashioned with a pattern-welded blade and steeled cutting edges to provide the most flexible and effective weapon. Sometimes the guards and pommel were embellished with elaborate cast or inlaid decoration in silver or brass. There is some variation in the form of the blades (a small minority of the early ones were single-sided) and in their technique of manufacture, which allows them to be classified, but the principal typology is based on the form of the guards and pommel (figure 3). Some may well have found their way into enemy hands before deposition — thus the discovery of an unassociated Viking-style sword is not necessarily a guide to the former presence of Vikings. A further complication is that good swords were treasured items, handed down from generation to generation; because of this, their loss is often most difficult to date accurately.

Careful microscopic examination of the swords sometimes provides further details about the scabbards in which they were

3. The more common types of Viking age sword hilts. (Drawn by G. Boyles.)

housed, although these have almost always rotted away. They usually had an outer leather sheath, within which were two wooden strips encased in textile, one on either side of the blade, each with an inner lining of wool. The scabbard's tip might be encased by a metal chape, both protective and decorative (figure 15). The sword's grip was usually of wood, sometimes bound with textile.

Much less expensive to produce than the sword was the spear. Normally its long wooden shaft does not survive, leaving only a socketed iron spearhead of gently curving 'leaf' shape or of a more angular form. Occasionally these too are decorated with inlaid wires around the socket, which is often pierced by a small rivet hole to allow fixing to the shaft.

A third main weapon was the iron axe, of which the head alone usually survives; again, there is a variety of forms. In addition to the sword, spear and axe a Viking warrior might have a bow and arrows, although these are not commonly found in graves; the arrowheads alone survive, leaf-shaped or angular, and either socketed or, more usually, tanged. A Viking might also carry a large single-sided knife, worn horizontally across his waist in a leather sheath.

The archaeological traces of defensive equipment usually amount to the circular iron umbo of a wooden shield. This consists of the raised hemispherical iron centrepiece and handgrip; the shield itself almost always rots away, although small iron fittings may be found. There is a unique instance at Ballateare, Isle of Man, of tiny fragments of the painted leather covering of a wooden shield, decorated with a simple pattern of narrow black and white stripes, enhanced with red dots. Otherwise no traces of

4. St Andrew's church, Middleton, North Yorkshire: a tenth-century warrior/settler wearing a helmet, with a knife across his waist, and with (to the viewer's right) a shield, sword and axe, and (to the left) a spear. (Photograph: A. Wiper. Copyright: R. Cramp.)

protective gear survive in the British Isles, for leather helmets rather than iron ones were normal (horned helmets were certainly *not* worn by Viking raiders), and leather jerkins probably protected the body (figure 4).

Viking fortifications

There is documentary evidence that some of the early Viking raiders had bases within the British Isles. In 866, for example, an Irish king took the offensive against 'pirate bases' on the northern coast from Donegal to Antrim, and there were probably other similar bases elsewhere from an even earlier date. Excavation in the Hebrides at the Udal, North Uist, has located what the excavator interprets as a small stone-built fort measuring only 7 metres (23 feet) across, dated approximately to the mid ninth century, and attributed to the Vikings. This unique structure was superseded by a tenth-century to eleventh-century settlement, apparently without substantial defences.

Although by the mid ninth century the Vikings had established permanent settlements in both Scotland and Ireland, it took longer for them to achieve this in England. If the documentary sources accurately reflect the pattern of summer raiding, it intensified after *c*.835, and a majority of the handful of places that could be called towns in turn fell victim, including *Hamwic* (Saxon Southampton), *Lundenwic* (Saxon London) and Canterbury. Viking raiders spent the winter in England for the first time in 850, when they based themselves on what was then the island of Thanet in Kent. In 854 they again overwintered, this time using another Kent island, Sheppey, while in 864 they reverted to Thanet as their winter retreat. No traces of Viking camps have been identified in either of these areas.

Towards the end of 865 a 'great army' of Vikings invaded. Precisely how many warriors there were in this 'great army' has been much debated. The long-established idea that it was many thousands, perhaps ten thousand, strong, was challenged in the 1970s when much smaller numbers, even as low as hundreds rather than thousands, were thought by some to be correct; now arguments are again being put forward to support the theory that several thousand warriors were involved. Certainty, however, seems impossible. After they had wintered in East Anglia the 'great army' captured York, their first triumph in what was to be a fourteen-year-long series of continuous campaigns in England. By 879-80 they were masters of the Yorkshire nucleus of the kingdom of Northumbria, the eastern half of the Mercian kingdom including the counties of Derbyshire, Leicestershire, Lincolnshire, Nottinghamshire, Bedfordshire, Cambridgeshire, Huntingdonshire and Northamptonshire, and the kingdom of East Anglia. The British kingdom of Strathclyde was also attacked in 874/5; its capital on the rock of Dumbarton, by the Clyde, had already been besieged and captured in 870/1 by the Dublin-based Viking army of Olaf 'the white'.

During its conquests the 'great army' occupied a variety of winter bases, which are recorded in the Anglo-Saxon Chronicle. Some, including London and Exeter, were old Roman sites with upstanding Roman fortifications. Others, such as Nottingham, are known to have been pre-existing Anglo-Saxon secular or religious foci, and a few, like Torksey, Lincolnshire, have no previous history. Repton, Derbyshire, where the Vikings over-

5. Repton, Derbyshire: plan of the Vikings' winter camp of 873-4 and the adjacent mass grave. (Drawn by G. Boyles, after Biddle.)

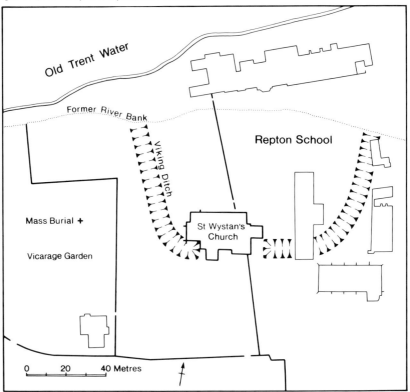

6. Repton, Derbyshire: the mass grave of 873-4 within the remains of a pre-Viking building, surrounded by the stone kerb of its covering cairn. Scale unit: 0.5 metre. (Photograph: M. Biddle.)

wintered in 873/4, is the only one of these places where the Viking encampment has been located, and even here the first indications were a chance by-product of an investigation of the notable Anglo-Saxon church. This building, which originated as a seventh- and eighth-century royal mausoleum for the kings of Mercia, stands close to the cliff edge of the old course of the river Trent. The church was commandeered by the Vikings as a stronghold, perhaps an entranceway, in the curved landward arm of a D-shaped enclosure (figure 5). This was defined by a rampart (no longer visible) and a ditch (now completely infilled), whose ends abutted the church. An area of approximately 0.5 ha (1¼ acres) was defended, but no traces of any contemporary occupation within the camp have so far been located, and the question of whether it accommodated the entire encamped army or was constructed only for use as an ultimate refuge for them should they be attacked remains open.

The Viking archaeology at Repton extends beyond the encampment to include what are provisionally interpreted as the skeletal remains of part of the 'great army'. Some 50 metres (55 yards) due west of the church, and outside the Viking defences, the remains of a derelict stone-built two-cell building provided the setting for a mass burial of some 250 individuals (figure 6). The bones were disarticulate when they were buried, with long bones stacked together and skulls placed on top. One possible explanation for this is that the bodies were originally buried or exposed elsewhere, allowing the flesh to come off, and that the bones were then collected together from their temporary repository for reburial here. The bones did not represent a true cross-section of a typical population but were from individuals aged almost exclusively in their late teens to forties, and the sexes were represented in a ratio of four men to one woman. None bore obvious marks of injury. All had been covered by a low cairn of stones, and then a mound of top-soil measuring 13 by 11 metres (42 by 36 feet) covered it all. When originally opened in the 1680s there was a record of a central stone coffin in what had been the eastern compartment of the building, but no trace of that remained.

The mass burial is dated by associated objects, including an axe, knives and other iron objects, and fragments of gold and silver. Most important are five pennies which all fit well with the overwintering date of 873/4. The form of burial, its date and the demographic characteristics of those buried combine to suggest that the mound's occupants were Vikings from the 'great army' and their womenfolk, but the absence of injury marks makes it likely that they were casualties of peace, perhaps of plague or disease, rather than of war. A possible, although less likely, alternative interpretation is that they represent a specially selected element of the local population who were killed for reasons of religion or retribution.

This mass burial is very different from a number of other Viking burials at Repton in the immediate vicinity of the church. One of these was accompanied by five silver pennies and a gold finger ring, found lying together beside the skull. Once again, the coins indicate a burial date in the 870s. Another skeleton, probably buried in a coffin, was accompanied by a sword in its fleece-lined leather-bound wooden scabbard, a folding knife, a silver Thor's hammer amulet and two glass beads at the neck, various buckles, a boar's tooth, and perhaps a wooden box between the legs; the skeleton was also noteworthy because it bore several indications of extreme violence. Still others, nearby, were each buried with an iron knife, and an axe dug up hereabouts by chance in 1922 probably came from yet another of these graves.

These remarkable discoveries will undoubtedly yield much more information when fully analysed, but they can be immediately recognised as the clearest evidence available for a range of the activities and personnel of the Viking 'great army'.

Early coin hoards

Coin hoards provide the earliest closely datable evidence for the Vikings' presence in Britain and Ireland. In these islands England alone had a coin-using and coin-issuing economy. A small number of hoards of English pennies buried *c.*800-50 is known: they have been found not only in England but also in Wales, Scotland and Ireland, but it is not possible to link the majority of them convincingly with Viking activity; they could just as well reflect inter-regional, local or personal uncertainties.

One contemporary hoard does, however, stand out through its composition as being of Viking origin. Found in 1871 at Mullaghboden, County Kildare, it consisted of eleven or more Carolingian silver *deniers* which combine to suggest that it was buried *c.*847; thus it was probably brought to Ireland by Vikings who had taken part in documented raids in France in 843-6.

The 'great army' of Viking warriors which was active in England in the period 865-80 had a more easily recognisable effect on the archaeological record. As they moved from region to region, initially as a single force but latterly in two separate

7. Arab *dirham* (diameter 30 mm, 1⅛ inches) representative of those found in Viking age hoards in Britain and Ireland. This example, a single find at 16-22 Coppergate, York, proclaims that it was struck for Isma'il Ibn Achmad at Samarkand in 903-7/8; but it is not an official silver issue but a contemporary forgery with a tin wash over a copper core. (Photograph: M. Duffy. Copyright: York Archaeological Trust.)

units, they inspired the burial of a spate of silver hoards. This is indicated by a steep rise in the number of hoards dated to these decades, which mostly contain English coins, and which in some cases can be matched quite accurately with the Vikings' documented movements.

One of the hoards, from Croydon, Surrey, buried in the early 870s, is the earliest British or Irish hoard to contain Kufic coins, which get their name because the style of their Arabic script is associated with the Mesopotamian city of Kufah (figure 7). With one exception, from a pre-Viking context in the Anglo-Saxon town of *Hamwic* (Southampton), these Islamic silver *dirhams* occur throughout the British Isles from the late ninth century and principally in the first half of the tenth century; they reached these islands from their minting places in the Near and Middle East via Scandinavian middlemen. These coins are therefore a tangible indication of Viking activity and, although it does not necessarily follow that they reached their points of loss in Scandinavian hands, this is likely to have happened in most cases.

4
The Scandinavian settlement

With the passage of time, the nature of the contact between the various races of the British Isles and their Scandinavian visitors changed, although this happened at different times in different places.

Scotland and the Isles

In the northern and western isles of Scotland raiding very soon gave way to immigration, with settlers from Scandinavia seizing political control and taking over the resources of land and sea. Areas of mainland Scotland, notably Caithness in the north-east and Dumfries and Galloway in the south-west, were also taken over in part by Scandinavian immigrants.

The earliest Norse settlements yet discovered, whether in Orkney, Shetland, the Hebrides or the Isle of Man, are difficult to date precisely but probably originated in the early decades of the ninth century. They appear to be the houses of immigrant farmers, who may also have gone raiding to supplement their income. Their buildings are rectangular in shape, and thus distinguishable from preceding native houses, which are based on circular or oval forms. Houses over 20 metres long and 6 metres wide (65 by 20 feet) are known; good examples can be seen at the well known site of Jarlshof, Sumburgh Head, Mainland, Shetland. The walls, which are slightly bowed, are normally defined by a quite well built, coursed rubble inner face and a rubble outer face, originally separated by a turf/earth core which gave both stability and warmth. Doors are often in opposed pairs, positioned off-centre in the long walls, and other characteristic features include long, axially placed stone-lined hearths set into the earth floor, and edge-set slabs defining 'sleeping benches' along the walls. The house sites often display a great complexity of superimposed walls for successive rebuildings and re-plannings, sometimes extending over many centuries (figure 8). Outbuildings, including byres, barns, smithies and such like, are also known, and coastal sites are sometimes accompanied by a *naust* or boathouse, such as that at Westness, Rousay, Orkney, built just above the water-line at a sheltered spot where boats could most easily be drawn up.

The overall settlement pattern, however, is a dispersed one, either of individual farms or occasionally, as at Jarlshof, of two or

8. Birsay, Mainland, Orkney. A building with curved walls overlying a rectangular structure at the Beachview site. (Photograph: C. D. Morris. Crown copyright.)

three houses and their outbuildings grouped together, perhaps representing an extended family unit. There is no evidence that these settlements were defended by ramparts or by any other means.

The standard assemblage of objects found in these buildings, and around them in the accumulations of domestic rubbish, most commonly includes items of bone or antler, such as dress pins, awls and combs, and sharpening stones. Spindle-whorls, line-sinkers for use in fishing, beads, lamps and large bowls were often made from the soft, easily worked soapstone or steatite, which was quarried on Shetland. Less frequently found, because they were more valuable and therefore rarer, more carefully looked-after and potentially recyclable, were items of bronze (again pins and other small items of personal adornment), of iron (knife blades, fish-hooks, strike-a-lights and sickles) and of glass (occasional beads). Pottery is also relatively uncommon, for the more durable and even repairable soapstone vessels had taken its place.

Ireland

Following the Vikings' early ninth-century settlements on Orkney and Shetland, on the Hebrides and perhaps on the Isle of Man, the next major land-taking was in Ireland, and here it is well documented and precisely dated. In 841 Vikings established what the Irish annalists described as a *longphort* at Annagassan, County Louth, and at Dublin. During the next half century further such *longphorts* were established at Cork (847), Waterford (pre-860), Youghal (pre-866), Limerick (pre-887) and Wexford and St Mullins (pre-892). Nearly all these coastal and riverine sites are now substantial towns, which presumably owe something of their development to the Vikings' impetus but, with the exception of Dublin, no trace of any Viking occupation or activity from this early period has yet been located at any of them.

It is not certain what exactly a *longphort* was, and the search for them is therefore so much the harder. Perhaps a relatively small fortified encampment was meant, much smaller than the tenth-century town which has been identified at Dublin, where excavations have as yet failed to unearth ninth-century remains. It seems increasingly likely, therefore, that the *longphort* there was some 2.5 km (1½ miles) upstream in the Islandbridge/Kilmainham area, where a large cemetery came to light during various building works and quarrying operations in the mid nineteenth century. At least sixty graves, and probably many more, must have been there originally, making it the largest Viking cemetery outside Scandinavia, but so limited are the nineteenth-century records that the great majority of the objects recovered from the skeletons have to be treated as unassociated finds. In the 1930s a further five graves were found at the nearby Longmeadows Park; three contained weapons, while the fourth was apparently accompanied only by a cow's jaw, and the fifth by two animal teeth. Although it is difficult to date any of the burials to within fifty years with any confidence, present opinion is that the Islandbridge/Kilmainham cemetery represents the dead of the ninth-century Dublin *longphort*.

England

In 876 part of the Viking 'great army' settled permanently in Northumbria and, in the words of the Anglo-Saxon Chronicle, 'proceeded to plough and to support themselves'. In 877 eastern Mercia was settled and in 880 East Anglia. This created the Danelaw, a territorial entity defined in a treaty between King Alfred and the Scandinavian king Guthrum in *c*.886-90. The boundary between 'English' England and Scandinavian England ran up the Thames, then up the Lea to its source, then in a straight line to Bedford, and then up the Ouse to Watling Street. To the north-east of this line Danish laws and customs prevailed, and to the south-west of it English ones.

The Danelaw boundary corresponds well with the limit of Scandinavian-influenced placenames in England. The commonest of these end in the elements *-by* ('village') or *-thorpe* ('hamlet') or have an English element such as *-ton* ('village') blended with a Scandinavian personal name such as *Grim* (the co-called 'Grimston hybrids'). There is also documentary evidence that after the Dublin Vikings were expelled from their *longphort* by the Irish in 902 some of them settled in and around the Wirral peninsula, and this is apparently confirmed by placenames of mixed Norse-Irish type in that vicinity. Despite the abundance of placename evidence in northern and eastern England, however, archaeological traces of this Scandinavian rural settlement are hard to find, presumably because the houses and farms they occupied are often buried beneath their modern counterparts. The only sizable body of archaeological evidence is the legacy of stone grave-markers, discussed in chapter 7.

These settlements and the treaty broke the mould of Viking activity and in a sense ended the 'classic' Viking period in England, the period of raiding and looting. Although there continued to be some sporadic raiding from abroad, and there are records of the newly planted immigrants sometimes raiding and attacking the English, the archaeological pattern in England should be transformed; we ought now to be looking for the farms, villages, towns and cities occupied by these no-longer-Vikings, although there are still their burials and the hoards of valuables signalling times of unrest to be sought out, as well as their influence on everyday items, jewellery, art styles and so on.

5
The development of towns

As there were apparently no towns in early Scotland, and since the early *longphort* at Dublin may not have been a town so much as a raiding base, the first towns to be developed by the Scandinavians in the British Isles were in England. Within the Danelaw the new settlers developed a number of regional centres which probably had administrative, commercial and defensive functions. In addition to York, which is discussed separately below, they included what are now the county towns of East Anglia and the eastern Midlands, and also Stamford. Nearly all of these places have produced some evidence for earlier occupation in the iron age, Roman, early Saxon or middle Saxon periods, yet the relatively short period of forty to fifty years that these sites were in Scandinavian hands before their recapture by the English in 914-18 may have been crucial in their evolution.

Archaeological traces of ditches that could represent defences of this era have been located only at Stamford and Nottingham, but it is not absolutely certain that they date to the period of Scandinavian control. The area enclosed by these defences at Nottingham is still unknown; at Stamford, although not yet fully defined, it seems to have been very small, approximately 1.1 ha (2.5 acres). This makes it only about twice the size of the Repton Viking camp, and indeed it could represent the Viking camp site of 868 or the defended nucleus of a pre-Viking estate, rather than having anything to do with real town life.

While under Norse rule, Stamford was a production centre for high-quality mass-produced pottery, wheel-thrown and sometimes glazed, but remains which can be dated to this period are minimal in virtually all the other centres. In the east Midlands only Lincoln has produced good evidence for the Scandinavian settlement and its impact; on a site at Flaxengate, deserted since the Roman period, new timber buildings fronting a new street system were laid out *c.*900, a foretaste of the further urban development that was to occur later in the century.

Coins

Although some coins were minted within Scandinavia in the early to mid ninth century, the Viking settlers of England found themselves in a more sophisticated coin-using economy than they were used to. For both propagandist and commercial reasons

9. Tenth-century silver pennies struck under Scandinavian auspices at York. (Top left) With religious mottoes *MIRABILIA FECIT* ('He has done wonderful things') and *DomiNuS DeuS Omnipotens REX* ('The Lord God Almighty is King') *c*.900. (Top right) 'St Peter' penny with sword and Thor's hammer motifs, *c*.925. (Centre left) King Olaf Guthfrithsson, *ANLAF CUNUNC*, with raven motif, *c*.940. (Centre right) King Sihtric Sihtricsson, with knot and standard motifs, *c*.942. (Bottom) King Eric Bloodaxe, with sword motif, 952-4. (Drawings copyright: York Archaeological Trust.)

they rapidly adopted the practice of minting coins themselves, and by the 880s silver pennies were being struck in the East Anglia and south-east Danelaw area with the legend 'St Edmund's money'. This was a remarkable circumstance, given that the Viking army had themselves killed the East Anglian king Edmund in 870. These coins conformed in general with the English currency, as did coins struck at York from *c*.890 (figure 9). Some of these early York issues bore the names of kings, while others carried the name of St Peter, and some had apparently nonsensical inscriptions which are believed to be made up from the initial letters of words in religious catch-phrases.

These religious mottoes were inherited from contemporary continental coins, but other 'words' on these coins have still to be deciphered, such as CUNNETTI, which appears on coins of *c*.900. To continue the ecclesiastical theme, Lincoln issued a series with the name St Martin in the 920s; by this time the moneyers of York were producing coins with more recognisably 'Viking' motifs such as swords and the Thor's hammer symbol. Although at times, depending on the political situation, English coins were more closely imitated, the most overtly independent Viking symbolism came with coins of Olaf Guthfrithsson, king of York in 939-41. He issued a coin with a bird emblem on one side, perhaps representing the raven associated, as a carrion eater, with the battle god Odin, and with its legend not in the Latin customary on contemporary English or even the previous independent 'Viking' issues, but with Old Norse used in its place. After 954, however, when Eric Bloodaxe, the last Scandinavian king, was expelled, York became part of mainstream English minting practice.

Dublin

Although the Vikings were expelled from the Dublin *longphort* in 902, a new Norse settlement at Dublin was founded in 917. It occupied about 10 ha (25 acres) on the south bank of the river Liffey, in the area, now including Christ Church cathedral and Dublin Castle, which became the later medieval town. Irregular in shape, it extended for 500 metres (550 yards) along the Liffey and for at least 200 metres (220 yards) back from it, with a succession of banks and revetments to the river. Beyond the commercial built-up centre lay the assembly place or *thing,* a Scandinavian name preserved in the name *Thingmote* given to a mound opposite St Andrew's church, which was removed only in 1685.

The street system within the central area included a principal spine road (Castle Street/Christchurch Place/High Street) intersected by roads running back from the river (Merchants' Hill/Nicholas Street). The lines of other thoroughfares, such as Winetavern Street and Fishamble Street, were dictated by the site's natural topography.

The areas excavated to date had been divided by fences into tenement plots, usually with buildings at or close to the street frontage (figure 10). It is these buildings which have received most of the detailed archaeological analysis so far. They are varieties of post and wattle structures, with the principal type averaging 8.5 by 4.75 metres (28 feet by 15 feet 6 inches) in size; it is not yet clear to what extent they reflect the Celtic building

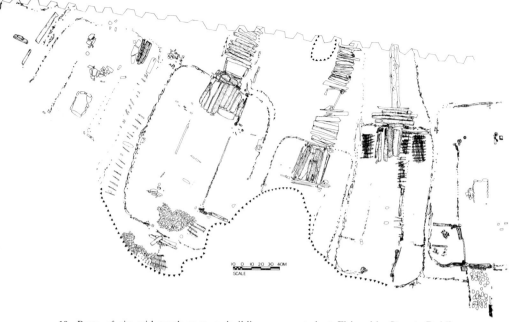

10. Parts of six mid tenth-century buildings excavated at Fishamble Street, Dublin. Planked paths lead to doors in the shorter walls of these sub-rectangular buildings, which have stake and wattle walls. Internally they are divided into three, with a central hearth. (Copyright: National Museum of Ireland.)

traditions of Ireland rather than those of Scandinavia.

Preliminary reports indicate that few of the associated objects are of specifically Scandinavian types, although British and continental items are present. Some of these arrived as the product of long-distance commerce, for Dublin served as the principal gateway to Ireland and as a centre for redistribution. Dublin's role was also as a manufacturing centre, and there is much debris from a variety of trades practised on an industrial scale. Among them was the working of bone and antler, leather, metals, textiles, wood, amber and lignite. The craftsmen were receptive to outside influences, whether in form, style or decoration, but they were catering principally for the native market in the city's hinterland. Nonetheless some types of object found in Dublin, notably the ringed pin for fastening clothing, are widely distributed across the Vikings' theatre of operations — the ringed pin also turns up in York (figure 11), Scandinavia, Iceland and even North America.

Despite this emphasis on trade and commerce, the Scandinavians in Ireland were content to make use of imported English coins until as late as 997 when Sihtric III Silkenbeard began to strike coins using English dies from the Watchet (Somerset), Worcester and Chester mints; some of the dies had been altered to include his own name or that of Dublin, or both.

11. Ringed pins of copper alloy from York. The longer pin measures 14 cm (5.5 inches). (Copyright: York Archaeological Trust.)

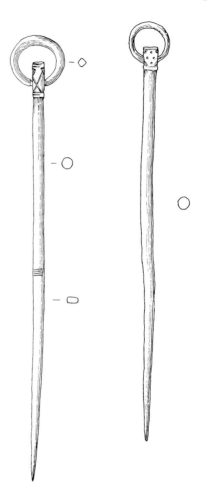

These dies were continuously copied, the imitations becoming increasingly unlike the originals, and English innovations in coin design were also successively mirrored at Dublin up to and beyond the Norman conquest of England. In turn, Dublin itself spawned a Manx coinage which seems to have started in much the same way that its parent's had done: Dublin dies were removed to the Isle of Man and were heavily used and copied in the period *c.*1025-75, although this series has no Manx mint name and no named Manx ruler.

York

In contrast to Dublin, York had a long pre-Viking urban history. It originated in a Roman foundation which had defended elements to either side of the river Ouse; during the Anglian period (400-850) these Roman enclosures had been largely abandoned for a site one kilometre downstream. During the Viking age there was resettlement in and around the Roman core areas, and a largely new street system, much of which was in being by the time the last Viking king was expelled in 954, was created. As at Dublin, the street plan appears essentially irregular, defined by a mixture of topographic and inherited historic features.

The Scandinavian presence in York, or *Jorvik* as it was then called, is shown by its street names, many of which incorporate the element -*gate,* derived from Old Norse *gata,* meaning street. Such names are not necessarily a sure sign of a Viking age origin, however, since the element remained current into the fourteenth century at least. Two other particularly evocative Old Norse names have survived to the present day. One is *Konungsgurtha,* 'Kings Court', now perpetuated as Kings Square, and perhaps indicating a Viking royal palace site based on the remains of the east gateway of the Roman fortress. The other is *Earlsburgh,* a pointer to the existence of a Viking age earls' residence in the vicinity of St Olave's church, which was itself founded by the penultimate Anglo-Scandinavian earl *c.*1030-55 and dedicated to the Norwegian patron saint, Olaf. These names indicate the seats of secular power in *Jorvik.* The position of the city's other major building, the cathedral church, has been located approximately by the discovery of its graveyard in the environs of the standing Norman and later medieval building, but no trace of it has yet been seen and excavation has shown that it does not lie beneath the present Minster.

In York, as in Dublin, properties were laid out and houses erected, but the buildings were constructed in a variant of the post and wattle tradition which is most likely to echo Anglo-Saxon practice (figure 12). They are rectangular, measuring 4 to 4.5 metres by at least 7 metres (13 feet to 14 feet 6 inches by 22 feet 9 inches), sometimes with evidence for wattle-lined benches along the walls and with a stone-lined and clay-based hearth, up to 2 metres (6 feet 6 inches) long, in the centre of the earth floor. Single-storeyed, their roofs were presumably of thatch. Later in the tenth century this type of building was replaced by a new form incorporating a semi-basement cut as much as 1.8 metres (6 feet) into the ground. Entered down a stone-lined passage, these

12. Post and wattle building of *c.*940 excavated at 16-22 Coppergate, York. Scale unit: 50 cm. (Photograph: M. Duffy. Copyright: York Archaeological Trust.)

rectangular structures, measuring on average 3.5 by 7.5 metres (11 feet by 24 feet 6 inches), were constructed of substantial oak planks, posts and beams. They usually had earth floors, although a single example of a plank floor resting on joists was discovered. This type of building seems to be one of the characteristic urban building forms of the ninth to eleventh centuries in England, although remains elsewhere survive only in 'ghost' form, all the timbers having decayed. Buildings of similar type have also been excavated in Dublin and Waterford, although there they are dated to a slightly later period, and in Dublin at least the type did not supplant the earlier post and wattle tradition.

The York range of manufactured items is much like that noted at Dublin (figure 13), and indeed in broad terms the everyday items found in both cities have much in common with each other and with those found in other north-west European towns. York did, however, stimulate the industrial production of pottery, a commodity seemingly not manufactured in Dublin. The pottery used in *Jorvik* was the local variant of a range of pottery forms including cooking pots, bowls, pitchers, lamps and so on, which

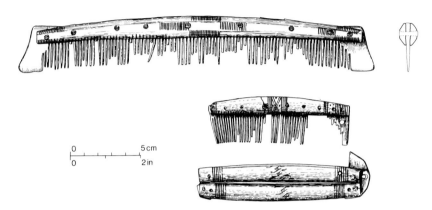

13. Antler combs and bone comb-case from York. (Copyright: York Archaeological Trust.)

was common throughout the Danelaw and beyond.

A most important feature of the groups of objects found in Dublin and York is that, because of the moist oxygen-free soil conditions in both cities, they include the items of wood, leather and textile which disappear to dust in normal, relatively dry soils. At a time when, for example, even glass vessels were luxury items, these and other slightly more resilient organic raw materials such as bone and antler played a vital role in the economy and everyday life.

In both Dublin and York the hands of Scandinavians can be clearly detected, and it is likely that excavation in other towns in both England and Ireland will eventually disclose indications of urban settlements of the Viking age and reveal more of their impact on the urbanisation of the British Isles.

6
Viking age art

The Scandinavian settlers of the ninth and tenth centuries brought with them not only distinctive types of jewellery, but also distinctive decorative forms and motifs. Some occur on items which were probably made in the Scandinavian homelands and transported to the British Isles, but it is clear that Scandinavian art styles were transplanted to at least some of the areas of Britain to which immigration took place. The Borre style, the earliest of these styles to become prevalent in Britain, has among its most easily recognisable elements what is called 'ring-chain' interlace. Famous examples are found on sculpture at Gosforth (Cumbria) (figure 20) and Andreas (Isle of Man). The style was also important in the Danelaw, notably at York, and it is represented not only on sculpture but also on metalwork and bonework (figure 14).

These insular (that is British) versions of the Borre style are not slavish copies of the Scandinavian original, however, and indeed some of the principal features which define the style in its Scandinavian form are largely missing in the insular variants. Once adopted and adapted, moreover, motifs such as ring chain could continue in fashion for a long time among more isolated or conservative schools of craftsmen, or indeed 'antique' features might come back into vogue; precise dating and stylistic definition can thus be difficult.

The second Scandinavian style to have a new lease of life in the British Isles was the Jellinge style. Its defining characteristic was animal ornament, with a long thin interlacing beast not dissimilar in some respects to some animal forms in contemporary insular art. An example of this style probably made in Scandinavia is an openwork scabbard chape from York (figure 15); York's own most notable use of Jellinge-style inspiration was by the metropolitan school of sculptors, who devised 'beast-chain' patterns incorporating Jellinge details.

In Scandinavia Jellinge animals developed into the fuller-bodied Mammen-style beasts, but this development appears to have made little impact on insular craftsmen, perhaps because it occurred at a time in the mid tenth century when direct contacts with Scandinavia had diminished. There are, however, some traces of the style in Britain, for example on sculpture at Braddan, Isle of Man (figure 16), and on silver brooches found at

14. Tenth-century knife found at Canterbury, Kent, but probably made in northern England. Its bone handle is decorated with Borre-style ring-chain (left face) and interlaced animals complicated by free rings (right face). Length: 103 mm (4 inches). (Copyright: Canterbury Archaeological Trust.)

Skaill in Orkney which were also, it has been suggested, made on the Isle of Man.

Towards the end of the tenth century, during the reign of Ethelred 'the Unready', England was once again invaded by Scandinavians, among them Olaf Tryggvason, later king of Norway, and Svein Forkbeard, king of Denmark. Svein's son Cnut (anglicised to Canute) eventually became king of England in 1016, and until 1042 England was ruled by him and then his sons. Their patronage, with that of their followers, inspired more Scandinavian influences, particularly on the arts.

These new influences, which embraced southern England much more comprehensively than any previous Scandinavian influence, have one of their best known and purest manifestations in a grave-marker found in 1852 in St Paul's Churchyard, London. A runic inscription on the side records that 'Ginna and Toki had this stone set up', and the face is decorated

15. Bronze openwork chape (end protector) for a sword scabbard, decorated with Jellinge-style animal interlace. Length: 87 mm (3½ inches). Found in Coppergate, York, 1906 and now in the Yorkshire Museum. (Drawn by D. Waterman.)

16. Odd's cross, Braddan, Isle of Man, showing two dragon beasts in Mammen style enmeshed in interlacing. The runic inscription reads: 'Odd raised this cross to the memory of Frakki his father, but Tho[rbjorn] . . .'. (Photograph: R. Trench-Jellicoe.)

in what is known as the Ringerike style (figure 17). The main feature of the design is a backward-looking beast, a further development of the earlier Jellinge and Mammen style animals of the later ninth and tenth centuries. Its neck and hips are formed as spirals, and it is entwined with tendrils which themselves end in another animal head. The design is accentuated by the survival of traces of blue-black, brown-yellow and white pigment, a useful reminder that detail could be applied in this way to what otherwise might seem to be relatively crude and simplistic carving. The beast's fuller body and the tendrils are among the features which distinguish Ringerike ornament from the earlier Scandinavian styles, and another characteristic is the pear-shaped lobe in each corner of the frame.

Combinations of variations on these features can be found on many small pieces of metalwork from southern England, particularly on the copper-alloy mounts which were riveted to book covers or boxes for their decorative effect. In many cases, how-

17. Gravestone with Ringerike-style decoration from St Paul's Churchyard, London. (Photograph: Museum of London.)

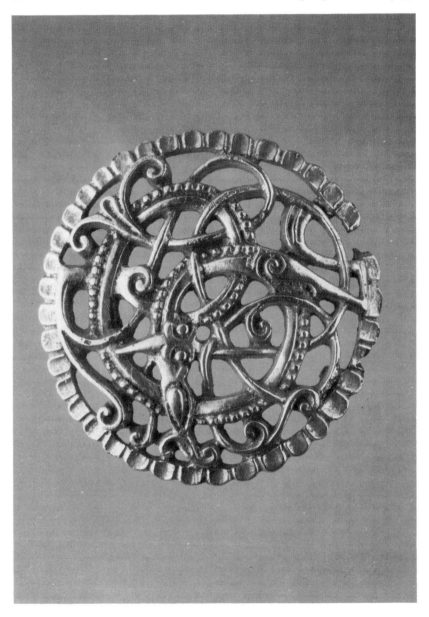

18. Gilt bronze brooch from Pitney, Somerset, in the Urnes style. Diameter: 39mm (1½ inches). (By courtesy of the Trustees of the British Museum.)

ever, art historians claim that these objects have affinities with the 'Winchester' school of Anglo-Saxon art, which shares the Ringerike taste for fleshy tendrils and lobe motifs. Such similar stylistic developments obviously promoted an appreciation of Scandinavian-derived pieces but can make it difficult to identify which have a predominantly Scandinavian influence and which owe most to English art.

It is clear, however, that Scandinavian influence on English art persisted even after the Danish royal line was replaced firstly by a descendant of the earlier Anglo-Saxon kings and then, after 1066, by Norman rulers. The last of the classic Scandinavian Viking age art styles, the Urnes style, with its characteristic entwined snake and ribbon-bodied animal, had a more limited impact on England but is reproduced on several brooches and other small pieces of metalwork. Among its finest expressions is a brooch from Pitney, Somerset (figure 18); unusual in its context is the example on a crosier found in the tomb of one of the Norman bishops of Durham.

These two final Viking age styles, the Ringerike and the Urnes, are also found in Ireland, particularly on material from Dublin. The series of excavations there since the early 1960s has brought to light a remarkable collection of carved wooden objects, unparalleled in variety and exuberance of decoration. While insular motifs of both English and Irish derivation play a major part in the repertoire of the carvers, some of the items display clear Scandinavian influence, although it may be that some of this influence reached Dublin by way of an English intermediary.

19. More typical of the nature of most Viking age sculptural remains than the complete stones illustrated elsewhere, this fragment, from Masham, North Yorkshire, shows a naked figure surrounded by serpents; it may represent Norse myth, contemporary propaganda or Christian allegory. Height: 55 cm (1 foot 9 inches). (Photograph: R. A. Hall.)

7
Stone carving

The custom of marking graves in churchyards with decorated stone memorials, either crosses or recumbent slabs, as opposed to stone settings, was one which the Scandinavians adopted from the English, and their enthusiasm led to the proliferation of sculptured monuments beyond the monasteries and more prestigious churches where previously they had been largely confined. Indeed, stone grave-markers of various types which show Scandinavian influence in their form and decoration are the commonest testimony to the Scandinavian settlement of northern and eastern England, although such influence does not automatically demonstrate the presence of Scandinavian settlers at the places where the sculpture is found. Unfortunately, too, virtually all of the sculpture is difficult to date to within fifty years. This problem is exacerbated by the fact that proliferation led to the production of some distinctly second-rate imitative work (figure 19).

The stones have often been found where they were later reused as building rubble, in parish churches, but there are two clear indications of their original purpose. In rare instances, most notably at York Minster and at St Mark's, Lincoln, examples have been found still in association with Viking age burials, while an example from Crowle, Humberside, has the Old English word *licbaecun*, literally 'corpse monument', that is 'memorial stone', carved on it in runes.

The Scandinavians brought to funerary sculpture their own artistic notions and decorative schemes. Some fragments, mostly cross shafts, depict Viking warriors with a selection of their weapons. The most famous example is at Middleton in North Yorkshire (figure 4), but there are several from other sites including Levisham (North Yorkshire), Weston (North Yorkshire) and Sockburn (Durham). Some of these figures may well represent the new Viking landlords who were enjoying the material rewards of their conquest and proclaiming the fact on their tombstones.

The mythological awareness of the sculptors or their patrons is particularly striking. Good examples are those representing scenes from the Sigurd saga, such as Sigurd roasting the heart of the dragon Fafnir and in the process burning his thumb, sucking it and thus being imbued with extra-sensory perception. All of this background would have come to the mind of a viewer seeing on a stone the single scene of a figure sucking his thumb, as portrayed on a fragment at Ripon, North Yorkshire. Other Sigurd scenes are depicted at Kirby Hill (North Yorkshire), York and Halton (Lancashire).

Another favourite story was of the smith Wayland. At Halton (Lancashire), he is depicted in his smithy, surrounded by his tools, and he is shown in another episode, fleeing from his royal captor by clinging to a bird, on crosses at Leeds (West Yorkshire) and Sherburn in Elmet and Bedale (both North Yorkshire). A fragment at Gosforth, Cumbria, shows the god Thor fishing for the World Serpent, and Gosforth also has a remarkably delicate and complete tall cross with scenes interpreted as *Ragnarök*, the doom of the Norse world, juxtaposed with a single explicitly Christian scene, the Crucifixion (figure 20).

In Scotland there is only one relevant stone, at Iona in the Hebrides. This shows human figures in a boat wielding swords and spears; above it, a smith and his tools probably represent one of the Scandinavian mythological scenes incorporating a smith, either Wayland, Regin or Sigurd, but much detail has been lost as a result of the poor condition of the shaft, and it is impossible to identify the scene with certainty.

On the Isle of Man, however, the predominant sculptural medium is slate, which is ideal for preserving the sculptor's intentions if not exposed too long to the weather, and there is a relative wealth of material, even if much of it is now fragmentary. This series, dated broadly to *c.*950-1000, includes several pieces showing scenes from the Sigurd story, and these are doubly important as being some of the earliest depictions of it (figure 21).

Both the Viking warrior representations noted earlier and the heroic mythological scenes were almost indisputably portrayed at the instigation of a Viking settler or his descendants. Some other decorative devices, including forms of animal ornament and patterns of knotwork or interlace, were clearly influenced by or derived from contemporary Scandinavian art, but their propagation cannot be so firmly attributed, as they passed into the shared repertoire of Anglo-Scandinavian sculptors.

These decorative forms also penetrated other areas. For example, the Anglo-Scandinavian sculptors of Chester exerted some influence on stone-carving in North Wales, with results such as the appearance of the ring-chain motif at Penmon, Anglesey, Gwynedd, or knotwork and fretwork patterns at Whitford, Clwyd. Scotland, however, remained virtually immune to

20. Gosforth, Cumbria: tenth-century cross with interlaced motifs and Norse mythological scenes. Height: 4.2 metres (14 feet). (Photograph: T. Middlemass. Copyright: R. Cramp.)

21. Andreas, Isle of Man. Sigurd bends over the triple-flamed fire to roast three rings cut from the dragon's heart. Above him are his horse Grani and the head of a bird. (Photograph: R. Trench-Jellicoe.)

Scandinavian styles in its sculptural tradition. In Ireland a monastic monopoly on the erection of crosses continued outside the influence of Scandinavian styles and fashions, and the Scandinavian coastal commercial settlements did not become foci for the art of stone sculpture in the manner of York. Only in the eleventh and twelfth centuries did Irish versions of the later Scandinavian art styles, the Ringerike and Urnes, appear sporadically in the sculptors' repertoire, and then most probably as a result of contacts between Ireland and England rather than through direct links with Scandinavia.

22. Hogback tombstones at Brompton, North Yorkshire. Average length: 1.3 metres (4 feet 3 inches). (Photograph: T. Middlemass. Copyright: R. Cramp.)

One novel type of grave-marker was created in the Scandinavian settlements of northern England, although it was probably a development from earlier Anglo-Saxon tomb slabs. This is the so-called hogback grave cover, characteristically a long, relatively narrow block of stone with a gently curving apex. In its classic version it looks like a stone model of a long-house with tegulated roof and schematic wall posts, and it has the remarkable feature of a muzzled bear clasping each end of the roof. The best collection of these hogbacks is in the church at Brompton, North Yorkshire (figure 22), and the largest number of fragments is at Lythe, North Yorkshire. Those at Penrith, Cumbria, are now arranged with a tall cross at each end and, although the details of this relationship are relatively recent, it may nonetheless show in broad terms how they were originally deployed. Their distribution is focused across northern England and southern Scotland, with only a few in the north Midlands, and one each in Cornwall, Wales and Ireland. There is a relatively late group in the Orkneys.

8
Runes

Runes are angular alphabetic letter forms, ideally suited for in-
cising on wood or cutting on stone; different varieties were used
by many Germanic peoples including the Scandinavians. The Isle
of Man has the densest distribution of runic inscriptions in the
whole Viking world, with about 26 substantial runestones surviving. Other Scandinavianised areas of Britain and Ireland have
only a relatively few, although the reasons for this disparity are
not clear. Runes were not confined to Viking settlers — the
Anglo-Saxons had written in runes since their own migration in
the fifth century AD and continued to do so during the Viking
age. Norse runic inscriptions are, however, distinguishable to the
expert by their letter forms and usages. Runic inscriptions continued to be carved beyond the end of the Viking age proper,
occurring, for example, on the twelfth-century font at Bridekirk,
Cumbria, or, more remarkably, cut by twelfth-century treasure-
hunters in the prehistoric burial mound at Maes Howe, Orkney,
which has the greatest concentration of runic inscriptions at any
one site in the British Isles. To recognise a runic inscription,
therefore, is not necessarily to recognise a work of the Viking
age.

Some Norse runic inscriptions occur on small portable objects.
They may boast of craftsmanship, as on a comb-case from Lincoln which proclaims 'Thorfastr makes a good comb' (figure 23).
Alternatively, they may proclaim ownership, like that on a sword
mount from Greenmount, Castlebellingham, County Louth,
which asserts 'Dufnall Sealshead owns this sword'. Similarly, an
eighth-century silver brooch from Hunterston, Ayrshire, Strathclyde, had an Old Norse runic text scratched on to it in the tenth
century which states that it was owned by Melbrigda, a man, like
Dufnall, with a Celtic name (figure 24).

23. Bone comb-case from Lincoln, with the runic inscription 'Thorfastr makes a good
comb'. Length: 132 mm (5¼ inches). (By courtesy of the Trustees of the British Museum.)

24. Hunterston, Ayrshire, Strathclyde: an early eighth-century silver brooch with the name Melbrigda scratched on the reverse in runes in the tenth century. Diameter: 122 mm (4¾ inches). (Photograph: National Museums of Scotland.)

Such cross-naming suggests contact and amalgamation between the Scandinavians and the native populations of the British Isles, and there are many similar instances in examples of the other category of runic inscriptions, those that are carved on large blocks of stone. The Manx runestones, which mainly belong to the tenth and eleventh centuries, were grave-markers, often with the inscription running up the narrow side of a slab, and sometimes with an inscription on the face, running upwards at one side of a central cross stem. Many of the inscriptions follow a set formula, 'A set up this cross in memory of B', and here again the Celtic and Norse names suggest a multiracial intermarried society.

9
Silver hoards

The Scandinavian settlement of north-west England introduced a new dimension into the politics of Northumbria by helping to promote a close political link between York and Dublin which lasted from the refounding of Dublin in 917 until York's final incorporation into the new state of England in 954. This was a period when the Dublin Vikings and the English kings of Wessex had a protracted struggle for supremacy in Northumbria; just as the fear of the earlier Viking raids had made people bury their valuables for safety, so too the turbulence of this period of intense rivalry for the throne of York led to the deposition of many more silver hoards in the countryside of northern England. In the tenth century many more hoards were also deposited in Scotland, Ireland, the Isle of Man and Wales, although not all of them need be directly linked to Scandinavian activity.

The earliest of these tenth-century hoards is the most remarkable, for it is four times larger than any other Viking hoard. Found in a lead chest by labourers repairing the bank of the river Ribble at Cuerdale, close to Clitheroe, Lancashire, in 1840, it consisted of about seven thousand coins and over thirteen hundred pieces of silver, mainly ingots, but including brooches and arm rings of Irish origin (figure 25) as well as some English, Carolingian and other jewellery. The coins in it are from three main sources, represented in the proportions 5:1:1. They are: firstly, the Viking kingdoms of eastern England; secondly, King Alfred's Wessex; and thirdly, the continent of Europe and other foreign sources. These foreign issues include Byzantine, Scandinavian, Islamic, Papal, North Italian and Carolingian coins, many of the last minted in Aquitaine, and perhaps acquired during the Viking raids there in 898. Together, they indicate that the hoard was buried c.903-5, and it seems to be the treasure of a Viking king or army.

Ingots and jewellery were both convenient forms in which to accumulate and, in the latter case, to display wealth; some ingots and simple arm rings seem to have been manufactured to conform to Scandinavian weight systems, but whenever necessary they could all be cut up into whatever weight of silver was required, and many of the Cuerdale ingots are cut fragments (hacksilver).

Many hoards contain complete or fragmentary examples of

25. Cuerdale, Lancashire: a portion of the early tenth-century silver hoard including coins, several forms of ingot, brooches, strap ends, Hiberno-Viking and other arm rings and hacksilver. (By courtesy of the Trustees of the British Museum.)

what are known as Hiberno-Viking arm rings. These are relatively thick bands of silver, rectangular in cross-section, tapering towards their ends, with stamped decoration on the outer face often incorporating a central diagonal cross (figure 25). They may be of Danish inspiration, but their overwhelmingly Irish distribution shows their principal place of manufacture, which occurred during the period c.850-950.

The Scotto-Viking version of these arm rings belongs mainly to the following century (c.950-1050). It is known as ring-money, for it is believed that the rings could have been used as currency — the Scottish tardiness in adopting a coin-using economy is a reflection of the relative unimportance of trade there as compared to Ireland and England. Ring-money comes in three main variants distinguished either by a circular cross-section with straight-cut terminals, or by a lozenge-shaped cross-section with either flattened spatulate or plain pointed terminals (figure 26). It circulated mainly in the Hebrides and Irish Sea area.

Silver brooches of Scottish, Irish or Pictish manufacture also occur in the hoards, either complete or as cut fragments (figures 24, 25, 26 and 28). There is a wide variety of decoration and size, but they consist essentially of a pin attached to a loop head which is either a complete circle (annular) or an almost complete circle (penannular). The extravagant size of some ball-type brooches (like those in the Skaill hoard, figure 26), and of their 'thistle brooch' antecedents which had brambled pinheads and terminals, demonstrates the desire for ostentatious display of wealth.

Other types of Viking age jewellery may also be found in hoards, including neck rings and arm rings and finger rings of twisted silver rods or plaited silver wires, arm rings and finger rings with stamped decoration, and arm rings of spiral rod form (the so-called Baltic or Permian type). Gold versions of some of these types are also known, but with the exception of the smallest class, the finger ring, they are very rare indeed; gold finger rings are merely 'rare'. Rare too are miniature Thor's hammer amulets, sometimes worn around the neck.

26. Skaill, Mainland, Orkney: part of the silver hoard deposited *c*.950, including Arab and English coins, the large ball-type penannular brooches, plaited neck rings and arm rings, Scotto-Viking 'ring-money' arm rings, and so on. (Photograph: National Museums of Scotland.)

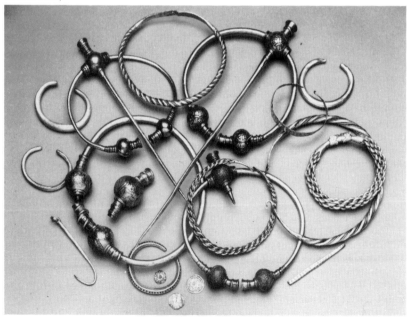

10
Graves

Norse burials have already been referred to, both in introducing some of the typical weapons and jewellery brought to the British Isles by Viking warriors and settlers, and also, in the case of the Islandbridge/Kilmainham cemetery in Dublin, to indicate the location of the early Viking *longphort*.

Graves are also where Viking age women are most clearly visible in the archaeological record. The image of the early raids as all-male events is not necessarily correct; the Repton mass burial hints otherwise, and the Anglo-Saxon Chronicle makes it clear that in 893 the leaders of an invading Viking army had their women and children with them. This may have occurred in earlier raids as well, but the grave finds that can be identified as those of Scandinavian females are more likely to belong to the period of settlement.

These burials are recognisable by a number of characteristic objects. Typical, although by no means ubiquitous, is the presence of a pair of characteristic oval brooches, sometimes known as 'tortoise' brooches (figure 27). These are cast in bronze, sometimes with openwork, and are decorated with elaborate stylised designs. Sometimes they were gilded to enhance their appearance. They were worn on the shoulders or breast, perhaps to hold together the back and front of an overgarment; a third brooch of different form was sometimes worn for decorative effect between them. Often these central brooches were trefoil-shaped, but there was a variety of forms; sometimes a piece of foreign metalwork, including pieces originally made to decorate Christian shrines or book covers, was adapted by the addition of a pin. Strings of beads, most often multicoloured glass or amber, are also commonly found in Viking age female burials (figure 28).

Brooches of typically Scandinavian form are, however, relatively rare in England and Ireland. For example, only about half a dozen pairs of oval brooches were found in the large ninth-century Dublin Viking cemetery at Islandbridge/Kilmainham, and there are only three other pairs from Ireland, while in England only three pairs are known. This may indicate that in early Viking Dublin and contemporary England there were relatively few native Scandinavian women. Rather more of these brooches have been found in Scotland and the Isles, however,

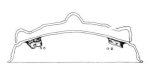

27. Oval ('tortoise') brooches from Bedale, North Yorkshire. (Top) Front view. (Centre) Side panel. (Bottom) Cross-section. Length: 11 cm (4.4 inches). (By courtesy of the Northumberland Estate and the National Museums of Scotland. Drawn by S. Howarth.)

28. Objects from the burial of a young woman with a probably new-born child at Westness, Rousay, Orkney, including one of a pair of oval brooches, a string of forty glass and other beads, two strap ends, a silver brooch, a comb, iron objects including a sickle (top left), one of two wool combs (top right) and shears (bottom left), a whalebone slab and a bone strip. An iron knife and a weaving batten are not shown. (Photograph: National Museums of Scotland.)

although not in the Isle of Man, the areas where there is less evidence for continuing long-term conflict between Vikings and natives, but more likelihood of widespread early settlement.

The graves are also of interest as archaeological monuments in their own right, for what they show of Viking age burial rites; and what they show is a diversity which reflects the great variety of Viking age burial forms and rituals known from Scandinavia, as well as some burial customs acquired within the British Isles. Unfortunately our knowledge is diminished by the fact that many of the cemeteries, including the large ones at Pierowall, Westray, Orkney, and at Islandbridge/Kilmainham, Dublin, as well as most of the richly furnished individual graves, were discovered in the nineteenth century, when techniques of excavation and recording were rudimentary by today's standards. However, starting with the excavations which Dr Gerhard Bersu undertook while interned during the Second World War on the Isle of Man, a corpus of more reliable information has been built up, including some remarkable discoveries.

The only cremation burials within the British Isles which have been attributed to Vikings or Scandinavian settlers are those at Ingleby (Derbyshire), where there is a cluster of insignificant mounds or barrows at the highest point in the area. On excavation some were identified as purely natural features, but others are clearly man-made, with a slight cairn of stones, surrounded by a stone kerb, covering a shallow earth mound. Some of the man-made mounds contained no sign of any cremation or inhumation burial and have therefore been interpreted as 'cenotaphs', but others sealed layers of burnt stones, charcoal, ash and bone. In some cases these were identified as cremation hearths. They contained only small fragments of human bone, but enough to suggest that some of the burials were those of women; bones of animals, thought to include sheep, ox, pig, horse and dog, were also found and interpreted as remains of grave-side feasts or gifts to the dead. Associated objects were few and found only in some graves; they included fragments of a sword, buckles, belt slides and nails, all in poor condition.

The Ingleby burials are the only certain Norse cremation burials in Britain, although burning did play at least a part in some of their other burial rites. At Hesket in the Forest, Cumbria, a cairn nearly 7 metres (23 feet) in diameter, on the line of the Carlisle to Penrith road, was partially removed in 1822. Below the stones, on a bed of fine sand, was a layer of charcoal, burnt bones and ashes, perhaps representing the site of a pyre rather than just fire debris, and in it was found a characteristically Viking collection of objects including a sword, two spearheads, an axehead, a shield boss, two spurs, a whetstone, an antler comb and (perhaps) its case, a horse bit and various buckles and strap slides (figure 2). Despite the presence of the comb fragments, which showed that bone/antler could survive in these soil conditions, there was no trace of a skeleton. The sword, which had silver-plated guards decorated with a ring-chain pattern suggesting insular manufacture, had been deliberately bent back on itself. This form of ritual 'killing' has been encountered at several sites and was perhaps carried out either to discourage grave-robbing, to help to lay the ghost of the deceased, or for some other ritual purpose. It was initially thought that all the metal objects in this grave had been burnt in a cremation pyre, which would account for the absence of a skeleton. More recently the corrosion products on these objects have been reassessed, and the theory that they were burnt has been questioned. Even if they were not, however, the layer of burnt material below the cairn attests a funeral fire, and at the least this may have been to consume the remains of animals, like those found with the Ingleby burials. Other instances of cremated animal bones occur in the upper layers of Viking/Scandinavian burial mounds on the Isle of Man, such as Balladoole, where horse, ox, pig, sheep/goat, dog and cat were recognised, and at Ballateare, where ox, sheep and dog were found.

Inhumation, not cremation, seems to have been the normal mode of Viking/Scandinavian burial in the British Isles, as it was for the preceding population, and some Scandinavian burials show the adoption of aspects of the local rite. It is not only their grave-markers which show the Scandinavian settlers of England adopting local Christian habits such as churchyard burial; occasional finds of distinctive artefacts in churchyards, such as a sword at Wensley, North Yorkshire, hint at accompanied churchyard burials like those at Repton (chapter 3). At the York parish church of St Mary Bishophill Junior two early to mid tenth-century burials have been located, one having a silver arm ring with a smaller silver ring attached to it on its upper left arm, and another accompanied by a knife, sharpening stone, buckle plate and coin. Even more remarkable, at Kildale, North Yorkshire a series of six or more burials was found in 1867, positioned head to toe just inside the nave north wall. They were accompanied by clothes fittings, weaponry and scales, although precise groupings were not recorded at the time of discovery; unfortunately the objects were later stolen from the church and not recovered.

There is an even denser concentration of churchyard finds, which may represent Viking burials, on the Isle of Man. In the churchyard at Jurby there is an unexcavated barrow, perhaps indicating a prestigious Viking burial, while excavations at St Patrick's Isle, Peel, have revealed Norse burials in the early Christian-medieval cemetery there, and several other graveyards have yielded weapons, either individually or sometimes in groups, which presumably indicate burials. These too point to an acceptance, albeit limited, of local traditions and practices.

In other cases apparently isolated Norse graves are positioned above or within a slightly earlier cemetery. A good example is the ship burial in its mound at Balladoole, Isle of Man. Here, however, both the earlier cemetery and the Viking grave lie within an earlier hillfort, which occupies a locally prominent position, and it may have been the site's commanding vantage point that was its main attraction. Certainly, elevated positions were often chosen for Viking/Scandinavian graves and form one main class of site, while another favourite location was on or near the seashore.

Wherever burial took place, the alignment of the grave and of the corpse within it do not seem to have followed a consistent pattern, and there is an equally great diversity in the position in which the corpse was laid to rest. Frequently it was placed on its back, legs extended, with the arms extended at the sides or meeting at the pelvis, but instances are known where the knees were drawn up or where the burial was crouched on its side.

The elaboration of burial ritual, at least in so far as it can be detected archaeologically, varied considerably. In some cases the corpse, accompanied by a selection of weapons, tools or jewellery, was apparently laid in a simple grave (figure 29). Sometimes a coffin or a wooden chest was used to contain the corpse; this may be detectable either through the presence of nails in appropriate positions, or through traces of wood preserved in the soil either as true timber or as a decayed discolouration. In some of the Manx burials there are wooden traces but no evidence of nails, an indication either that the coffin or container was jointed together, or that the timbers may have formed a simple plank lining to the grave pit.

Sometimes the body was placed in a stone setting rather than in a wooden container. One-piece stone coffins were not used; instead, the common technique was to construct a coffin-shaped

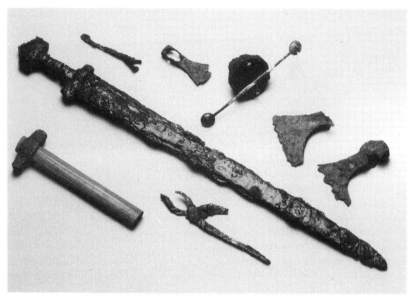

29. Sword, axes, shield fittings, an adze, a hammerhead (remounted), shears and an unidentified iron strip from the man's grave at Ballinaby, Islay, Hebrides. (Photograph: National Museums of Scotland.)

container, called a cist, from slab-like stones. This custom was already used in some of the Christian communities which the Scandinavian immigrants took over, and indeed it continued in use during and after the Viking age. It is therefore not in itself an indicator of a Norse burial, which can be confirmed only by the presence of typical grave goods.

Probably the most remarkable Norse cist or lintel grave in the British Isles is that found in 1984 in the Christian cemetery to the north of St German's cathedral on St Patrick's Isle, Peel, Isle of Man. The grave was that of a middle-aged female, and careful excavation revealed an unusually varied group of accompanying objects which proclaim her Scandinavian associations. Notably, she did *not* have a pair of oval brooches, the classic hallmark of a Norse woman's burial; instead, her jewellery consisted of a neck-lace of glass, amber and jet beads, while two larger beads, of amber, were found at the waist, as was an ammonite fossil, per-haps an amulet. Other items buried with her were an antler comb, a pouch of leather and bronze containing two bronze needles, three iron knives with wooden hilts, some of them decorated with silver wire, iron shears with associated cloth remains, and an iron cooking spit which had been wrapped in cloth of at least four types. Remains of feathers, perhaps of goose, were also attached to the spit. The only indicator of date is provided indirectly by another, adjacent, grave in which there was a coin of the English king Edmund (939-46); this suggests that accompanied burial was current on St Patrick's Isle into the mid tenth century.

Norse cist burials sometimes occur within or below mounds, for example at Aspatria, Cumbria, while others lie below a stone setting of some form. An example of this is at Talacre, at the northern tip of the Dee estuary in Clwyd, where a cist made from three stones at each side, one at each end, and with a stone slab lid, lay 1.8 metres (6 feet) below and 1.8 metres to the north of a setting of stones arranged to form a pointed oval measuring 1.4 by 0.3 metres (4 feet 6 inches by 1 foot). This setting, which could be described as ship-shaped, appears to have been only a marker, but at Westness, Rousay, Orkney, at least two oval stone-lined graves have been found, which may also represent a variant of boat burial. One of them has a higher stone at one end which, if this interpretation is correct, may represent a ship's prow.

Boats containing the corpse are known from just a few Viking/ Scandinavian burials in the British Isles, but, like the wooden coffins or containers, their timbers have rotted away. They have therefore been recognised by the discovery of concentrations of clench nails, a type of nail with a large head and a rove, often diamond-shaped, between which the overlapping planks of the clinker-built boats could be secured. When the boat's timbers decay the clench nails usually remain more or less in their respective positions, held in place by the soil within and around the boat, and if they are not disturbed by burrowing animals they can be exposed by meticulous excavation to present a coherent picture of the ghost vessel. Less cautious excavation, such as that which brought to light a concentration of clench nails in a mound at Kiloran Bay, Colonsay, Hebrides, in 1882-3, does not allow the shape of the boat to be recovered; this was a rich male burial, accompanied by, among other things, Northumbrian coins of the mid ninth century, which provide an unusually clear indication of the date of burial (figure 30).

There are similarly tantalising indications of boat burials at a number of sites in the western and northern isles of Scotland, but in most cases the crude methods of investigation and recording did not result in the boat's form being recovered; one of these poorly

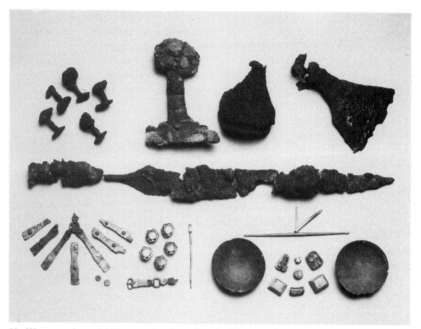

30. Weapons (sword hilt, spearhead, axehead, shield boss), harness gear (bottom left), scales, pans and decorated weights (bottom right) and clench nails (top left) from a male burial at Kiloran Bay, Colonsay, Hebrides. (Photograph: National Museums of Scotland.)

investigated sites, on the Hebridean island of Oronsay, was notable for containing both a male and a female skeleton, apparently buried simultaneously. Somewhat better was the excavation carried out at Knoc-y-doonee, Isle of Man, in 1927, where at least there is a record that the clench nails covered an area of approximately 8.5 to 9.1 metres by 1.8 to 2.4 metres (28 to 30 feet by 6 to 8 feet), while at another Manx site, Balladoole, the nails indicated a boat measuring some 11 by 3 metres (36 by 10 feet).

At Westness, Rousay, Orkney, however, two boat burials, 4.5 and 5.5 metres (14 feet 9 inches and 18 feet) long, have been found and recorded in much more detail (cover illustration). Each had a burial chamber amidships, defined by large flat stones and containing a male burial. And at Scar, Sanday, Orkney, excavation in 1992 revealed remains of an old woman, a man and a child, all in one boat; the many grave goods included a superb whalebone plaque, jewellery and weapons.

Mounds or cairns are a common feature of Viking/Scandinavian burials, and it is clear that considerable care could be taken in their construction. At Ballateare, Isle of Man, the mound was made of turves, apparently brought from some distance, while the one covering the Knoc-y-doonee boat burial had been carefully capped with white stones, and that at Balladoole may have had a marker post of some sort erected on its top — a 60 cm (2 foot) deep post hole, to hold a wooden upright, was apparently contemporary with the burial.

Sometimes, however, mounds may not be what they initially seem, particularly at sandy beach-side sites, where sand-blow can create dunes which may by chance cover a grave and give it the appearance of a mound cover. Conversely, these natural agencies may have sometimes removed sandy mounds from over graves, leaving them to appear, on discovery, as simple unmarked burials.

Again, prehistoric or natural mounds seem sometimes to have acted as a focus for Viking/Scandinavian graves, which may be positioned between pre-existing mounds or inserted into their top or side as what are called 'secondary burials'. A good example is the cemetery found in the nineteenth century at Pierowall, Westray, Orkney, and the records of a find in 1822 at Claughton Hall, Lancashire, suggest that the Scandinavian burial there may have been inserted into a bronze age mound. Finally, there is also room for confusion because mound burial was a custom of some indigenous British peoples, for example the Picts of Scotland. Although the Scandinavians sometimes took over a Pictish settlement and left their recognisable imprint on its archaeology, it must not be assumed that any nearby mounds represent Scandinavian rather than Pictish burials.

Another aspect of Norse burial rites in the British Isles is the occasional occurrence of double burials of male and female. At Santon Downham, Norfolk, a grave found in 1867 reportedly contained a male, accompanied by a sword, and a female identified by a pair of oval brooches; the grave goods suggest that they could have been a Scandinavian couple who died simultaneously, presumably from natural causes. The Claughton Hall (Lancashire) burial, found in 1822 and only sketchily recorded, may have been another similar instance, but not all double burials were so benign. At Ballateare, Isle of Man, a female skeleton with a slashed skull, but without any accompanying grave goods, was found in the upper part of the mound which contained a rich male burial; this looks like a case of ritual sacrifice. More ambiguous traces of what could nonetheless be another instance are provided by female bones found in another Manx burial mound, at Balladoole, and the records of two female skeletons found at the feet of a warrior burial at Donnybrook, Dublin, could be yet another example of a custom which is known from Viking age Scandinavia.

Most of the items regularly found in British Viking/ Scandinavian burials have been mentioned in discussing the various burial rituals, but there are a few others which deserve notice. Sickles are occasionally found, occurring in both male and female burials, and can be interpreted as a recognition of the agricultural activities of the Scandinavian settlers. Bronze balances with hinged folding arms and their pans, chains and lead weights reflect exchange, possibly commercial, and the sporadic finds of smiths' hammers and tongs are a reminder of the importance of the metalworker in Viking age society. The horse skeletons and riding gear found in several graves are probably to be interpreted as additional indicators of the prestige and wealth of the deceased.

11
Epilogue

The final major Scandinavian assault on England was that by King Harald Hardraada of Norway in 1066, which ended with his defeat and death at the battle of Stamford Bridge, some 11 km (7 miles) east-north-east of York. But Danish fleets were around the English coast in 1069 and 1075, and Magnus Barelegs of Norway was active in Wales, Scotland and Ireland at the end of the eleventh century. These contacts persisted, with the Isle of Man and the Western Isles remaining under Scandinavian overlordship until 1266, and Orkney and Shetland as late as 1469, but the archaeology of this period is in many respects different from that of the formative period, the Viking age proper.

12
Museums and sites

The main museum collections and displays of Viking age objects in Britain and Ireland are listed here. In addition, many county museums throughout the English Danelaw also display some material.

The British Museum, Great Russell Street, London WC1B 3DG. Telephone: 0171-636 1555.

Jorvik Viking Centre, Coppergate, York, North Yorkshire YO1 1NT. Telephone: 01904 643211. Portrays an archaeologically based recreation of life in a Viking age town, the well-preserved remains of tenth-century timber buildings and a selection of artefacts.

Manx Museum, Douglas, Isle of Man IM1 3LY. Telephone: 01624 675522.

Museum of London, London Wall, London EC2Y 5HN. Telephone: 0171-600 3699.

National Museum of Ireland, Kildare Street, Dublin 2, Republic of Ireland. Telephone: 01-6618811.

Royal Museum of Scotland (Museum of Antiquities), Queen Street, Edinburgh EH2 1JD. Telephone: 0131-225 7534.

Shetland Museum, Lower Hillhead, Lerwick, Shetland ZE1 0EL. Telephone: 01595 5057.

Tankerness House Museum, Broad Street, Kirkwall, Orkney KW15 1DH. Telephone: 01856 3191.

Tullie House Museum and Art Gallery, Castle Street, Carlisle, Cumbria CA3 8TP. Telephone: 01228 34781.

Yorkshire Museum, Museum Gardens, York, North Yorkshire YO1 2DR. Telephone: 01904 629745.

The areas where a variety of Norse archaeological sites is most readily visited are the Isle of Man, Orkney and Shetland. For Orkney, note that boat services to the outlying islands are not on a daily basis; it is therefore necessary to plan carefully or to fly. On Mainland, Orkney, coach tours throughout the summer give access to many of the notable sites; on Shetland, private transport is more desirable. Useful contact addresses include the Isle of Man Department of Tourism, Sea Terminal Building, Peveril Square, Douglas, Isle of Man IM1 2RG; Orkney Tourist Organisation, Information Centre, Kirkwall, Orkney KW15 1DE; Shetland Tourist Organisation, Information Centre, Lerwick, Shetland ZE1 0LU.

In England, Yorkshire and Cumbria in particular provide plentiful opportunities to see Viking age sculpture, and some of the most important find spots have been referred to. Where the text specifies that sculpture is *at* a site, then it is currently still there, but beware, because sculpture from some sites has been removed elsewhere for safe-keeping. The church which formed part of the Repton (Derbyshire) camp site may also be visited; most of the camp area is on the private land of Repton School, where there is nothing of this period to be seen.

The ARC (Archaeological Resource Centre), St Saviourgate, York, opened in 1990 and provides pre-booked school parties with an opportunity to try their hands at a variety of Viking age crafts, including weaving and leatherworking, as well as other archaeological skills and a computer-aided exploration of the 'Viking Dig' site, all in the context of a working archaeological unit. For further details telephone: 01904 654324.

For viewing at home or in school
The World of the Vikings, a compilation of 3500 colour photographs with spoken commentary, supported by computerised indexes, glossary and maps, is available as a CD-Rom disc or, with additional video sequences illustrating Viking crafts, on laser videodisc. It originated as a joint York Archaeological Trust/National Museum of Denmark project. For further information, contact Past Forward Ltd, Piccadilly House, 55 Piccadilly, York YO1 1PL. Telephone: 01904 670825 or 670826.

13
Further reading

Bailey, R. N. *Viking Age Sculpture.* Collins, 1980. Analyses development, sources, schools, decoration, iconography and production, principally in northern England.

Baldwin, J. R., and Whyte, I. D. (editors). *The Scandinavians in Cumbria.* Scottish Society for Northern Studies, Edinburgh, 1985. Scholarly essays on a variety of topics.

Batey, C. E., *et al* (editors). *The Viking Age in Caithness, Orkney and the North Atlantic.* Edinburgh University Press, 1993. Various scholarly essays.

Crawford, B. E. *Scandinavian Scotland.* Leicester University Press, 1987. Multi-disciplinary approach, including late Norse material.

Fell, C., *et al* (editors). *The Viking Age in the Isle of Man.* Viking Society for Northern Research, London, 1983. Various scholarly essays.

Graham-Campbell, J. (editor). *Viking Age Treasure from the North West* [England]. Liverpool Museum, 1992. Essays discussing the Cuerdale hoard.

Hall, R. A. *The Viking Dig.* Bodley Head, 1984. First impressions of the Viking age (and other) discoveries in Coppergate, York. Many illustrations.

Hall, R. A. *Viking Age York.* Batsford, 1994. General introduction with many illustrations.

Lang, J. T. *Anglo-Saxon Sculpture.* Shire, 1988. Concise illustrated introduction including pre-Viking material.

Loyn, H. R. *The Vikings in Britain.* Batsford, 1977. Historical narrative of the period.

Page, R. I. *Runes.* British Museum Publications, 1987. Short, well-illustrated introduction.

Richards, J. D. *Viking Age England.* Batsford, 1991. Archaeologically focused introduction with many illustrations; includes Isle of Man.

Ritchie, A. *Viking Scotland.* Batsford, 1993. Archaeologically focused introduction with many illustrations.

Roesdahl, E. (editor). *The Vikings in England.* Anglo-Danish Viking Project, London, 1981. Short topic essays with profuse illustration.

Index

Page numbers in italics refer to illustrations